HOW TO LIVE A
BLESSED LIFE

PRINCIPLES FROM
THE LIFE OF THE
RIGHTEOUS MAN
IN PSALM 112

BRIAN HOUSTON

PUBLISHED BY MAXIMISED LEADERSHIP

How to live a blessed life
First published February 2002
Second printing May 2002

Copyright © 2002 Brian Houston
All rights reserved. No part of this publication may be
reproduced in any form or by any means without prior written
permission from the publisher.

> Houston, Brian
> ISBN 0 9577336 3 1

Scripture quotations used in this book are from the following
sources and used with permission:
New King James Version (NKJV). Copyright © 1982, 1992 by
Thomas Nelson, Inc. Used by permission. All rights reserved.
The Amplified Bible (AMP). Old Testament Copyright ©
1965,1987 by the Zondervan Corporation. New Testament
Copyright © 1958, 1987 by the Lockman Foundation. Used by
permission.

Emphasis in certain scriptures is the author's own.

Back cover photo of Brian Houston by Femia Shirtliff
Inside photos by Bobbie Houston

Printed by J S McMillan Printing Group, Sydney Australia

Published by Maximised Leadership,
PO Box 1195, Castle Hill, NSW 1765 Australia
www.maximisedleadership.com

DEDICATION

8/15/03

For Jim,
Be blessed!
Love,
The Cobarrubias Family
Jon, Porpha, Joni & Josiah

raise the Lord! Blessed is the man who fears the Lord, who delights greatly in His commandments. ² His descend
will be mighty on earth; The generation of the upright will be blessed. ³ Wealth and riches will be in his house, and
righteousness endures forever. ⁴ Unto the upright there arises light in the darkness; He is gracious, and full of com
ion, and righteous. ⁵ A good man deals graciously and lends; He will guide his affairs with discretion. ⁶ Surely he
never be shaken; The righteous will be in everlasting remembrance. ⁷ He will not be afraid of evil tidings; His hea
teadfast, trusting in the Lord. ⁸ His heart is established; He will not be afraid, until he sees his desire upon his ener
⁹ He has dispersed abroad, He has given to the poor; His righteousness endures forever; His horn will be exalted
onour. ¹⁰ The wicked will see it and be grieved; He will gnash his teeth and melt away; The desire of the wicked
erish. Praise the Lord! Blessed is the man who fears the Lord, who delights greatly in His commandments. ²
escendants will be mighty on earth; The generation of the upright will be blessed. ³ Wealth and riches will be in his ho
nd his righteousness endures forever. ⁴ Unto the upright there arises light in the darkness; He is gracious, and fu
ompassion, and righteous. ⁵ A good man deals graciously and lends; He will guide his affairs with discretion. ⁶ Su
e will never be shaken; The righteous ot be afraid of evil tidings; His
s steadfast, trusting in the Lord. d, until he sees his desire upon
nemies. ⁹ He has dispersed abroad, ures forever; His horn will be exa
with honour. ¹⁰ The wicked will see it lt away; The desire of the wicked s
erish. Praise the Lord! Blessed i eatly in His commandments. ²
escendants will be mighty on earth; ealth and riches will be in his ho
nd his righteousness endures foreve darkness; He is gracious, and fu
ompassion, and righteous. ⁵ A good his affairs with discretion. ⁶ Su
e will never be shaken; The righteou ot be afraid of evil tidings; His
s steadfast, trusting in the Lord. d, until he sees his desire upon
nemies. ⁹ He has dispersed abroad, ures forever; His horn will be exa
with honour. ¹⁰ The wicked will see it lt away; The desire of the wicked s
erish. Praise the Lord! Blessed is the man who fears the Lord, who delights greatly in His commandments. ²
escendants will be mighty on earth; The generation of the upright will be blessed. ³ Wealth and riches will be in his ho
nd his righteousness endures forever. ⁴ Unto the upright there arises light in the darkness; He is gracious, and fu
ompassion, and righteous. ⁵ A good man deals graciously and lends; He will guide his affairs with discretion. ⁶ Su
e will never be shaken; The righteous will be in everlasting remembrance. ⁷ He will not be afraid of evil tidings; His
s steadfast, trusting in the Lord. ⁸ His heart is established; He will not be afraid, until he sees his desire upon
nemies. ⁹ He has dispersed abroad, He has given to the poor; His righteousness endures forever; His horn will be exa
vith honour. ¹⁰ The wicked will see it and be grieved; He will gnash his teeth and melt away; The desire of the wicked s
erish. Praise the Lord! Blessed is the man who fears the Lord, who delights greatly in His commandments. ²
escendants will be mighty on earth; The generation of the upright will be blessed. ³ Wealth and riches will be in his ho
nd his righteousness endures forever. ⁴ Unto the upright there arises light in the darkness; He is gracious, and fu
ompassion, and righteous. ⁵ A good man deals graciously and lends; He will guide his affairs with discretion. ⁶ Su

How to live a blessed life – I believe that is what every human being needs to know. Yet the reality is that there is already a book in existence that gives all the instruction you need. It is the most widely read, most often translated and best-selling book of all time. If you haven't guessed it, that book is the Bible.

There are some who think that the Bible is dull and irrelevant, full of rules and regulations. Sadly, that presumption causes them to miss out on the wealth of truth, information and understanding about God and life that the Bible contains.

As God's Word to us, it has all the wisdom we need for living life successfully. It covers everything – from health, finance, business and work, to relationships, marriage and parenting – anything and everything you could ever want to know. No matter how many times you read it, there is always something new and relevant for whatever circumstance you are facing.

The Bible is my manual for living. It embraces every aspect of life and I've given my life to teaching its principles to others.

Among the diverse range of colourful characters in the Old Testament, there is one I particularly admire and aspire to most of all. I love his thinking and approach to life. His name isn't mentioned, but he lives by Bible principles and in ten verses of scripture, you read how God's blessing crosses the spectrum of his life.

This Bible hero of mine is the righteous man described in Psalm 112, and by applying some of the key principles with which he conducts his life, we can live a blessed life too.

PSALM 112

P raise the Lord! Blessed is the man who fears the Lord, who delights greatly in His commandments.

2. His descendants will be mighty on earth; the generation of the upright will be blessed.

3. Wealth and riches will be in his house, and his righteousness endures forever.

4. Unto the upright there arises light in the darkness; he is gracious, and full of compassion, and righteous.

5. A good man deals graciously and lends; he will guide his affairs with discretion.

6. Surely he will never be shaken; the righteous will be in everlasting remembrance.

7. He will not be afraid of evil tidings; his heart is steadfast, trusting in the Lord.

8. His heart is established; he will not be afraid, until he sees his desire upon his enemies.

9. He has dispersed abroad, he has given to the poor; his righteousness endures forever; his horn will be exalted with honour.

10. The wicked will see it and be grieved; he will gnash his teeth and melt away; the desire of the wicked shall perish.

'PRAISE THE LORD!'

[PSALM 112:1]

PRAISE THE LORD

Praise the Lord! Within those three words is the powerful *beginning* and *foundation* of a blessed life. It starts with knowing who God is and praising Him.

Praise is always a starting point. It means thankfulness – that is why we give thanks *before* a meal and *start* church with songs of praise. Jesus began to thank God before Lazarus was raised from the dead, and Moses praised God before He parted the Red Sea. Human nature likes to wait until after an answer is received, but blessing *begins* with praise.

The Word of God tells us to 'enter His gates with *thanksgiving* and into His courts with *praise*' (Psalm 100:4). Yet praising the Lord is not limited to singing a few songs once a week in a church service. Worship is a lifestyle that embraces the entire spectrum of life. You can praise God at any hour of the day, seven days a week – in the car, in the shower or in the middle of night. It isn't about singing a particular hymn or reciting a prayer – it's about a relationship with your Heavenly Father who loves and cares for you.

People have different ideas of what God is like and they communicate with Him according to their perception. Those who think He is rigid and austere keep their distance. Others who see Him as formal and stiff, usually approach Him in the same way. Yet those who know Him as Father and Friend enjoy the blessing of a close, intimate relationship with Him – where you can call Him any time.

No matter what situation you may be in, you are not alone. Circumstances begin to turn around when you start praising God. Not only does it put Him in focus, but it causes you to see things from a whole new perspective. When He becomes the focus of your life, things begin to change for the better.

'BLESSED IS
THE MAN
WHO FEARS
THE LORD.'

[PSALM 112:1]

BLESSING

'*Blessed (happy, fortunate, to be envied) is the man who fears (reveres and worships the Lord)*' is the way the Amplified Bible translates the first verse of Psalm 112.

Throughout the Bible, God consistently promises to *bless* His people, but His blessing also depends on our choices. He puts two clear choices before people:

> '*I have set before you life and death, **blessing and cursing**; therefore choose life, that both you and your descendants may live.*'
>
> (Deuteronomy 30:19)

The book of Deuteronomy in the Old Testament contains a list of blessings and a list of curses which were directly linked to whether one chose to obey or disobey the commandments of the Lord. You can read these in Deuteronomy 28:1-14. To choose life with God is to choose a blessed life.

God's will is always to bless you, but if you think His blessing is entirely for you, you are missing the point. The blessing of God in your life should go well beyond your own existence.

God told Abraham that He would bless him, but the purpose of blessing him went far beyond his own life. This is what God said:

> '*I will make you a great nation; I will bless you and make your name great; and **you shall be a blessing**.*' (Genesis 12:2)

The purpose of God's blessing is to enable you to be a great channel of blessing to others. If you have *nothing*, there is nothing you can do for anyone else; if you have a *little*, you can only help a little; but if you have a *lot*, there is a whole lot you can do. When you are blessed, you have a mighty foundation from which to impact others. You are blessed to be a blessing.

'WHO DELIGHTS
GREATLY IN HIS
COMMANDMENTS'

[PSALM 112:1]

THE WORD

You will only enjoy the Bible's promises if you choose to live by Bible principles. Everyone wants to be blessed, but not everyone is prepared to live by the conditions or principles that bring about God's blessing. Simply put, if you want Bible results, you have to live by Bible rules.

Psalm 112 tells us that the righteous man 'delights greatly' in God's commandments. He loves the Word of God and has made it the foundation on which he builds his life. The result is a life which is a candidate for blessing in every area – relationships, finance, career, social life, family and spiritual life.

Living according to God's Word is not a selective process that allows you to choose to live by some commandments but not others. The Bible says:

*'This Book of the Law shall not depart from your mouth, but you shall meditate on it day and night, that you may observe to do according to **all** that is written in it. For then you will make your way prosperous, and then you shall have good success.'* (Joshua 1:8)

If you want to live a blessed life, understand that the key is to observe to **do** according to all that is written in the Bible. One might be impressed with someone who *knows* what the Bible says, but it is much more impressive to see its promises actively blessing someone's life.

The blessed man in Psalm 112 took delight in God's Word because he saw it working in his life. In the New Testament, James encourages us to 'be doers of the Word, not hearers only' (James 1:22). You can faithfully 'attend' church or listen to sermons but unless you apply the principles, you will not experience the kind of blessing God intends for your life.

'HIS DESCENDANTS WILL BE MIGHTY ON EARTH.'

[PSALM 112:2]

IMPACT and INFLUENCE

Your life is a lot bigger than you might think it is. Not only are you blessed to be a blessing to others, but you are also setting the pattern or example which others will follow. The Apostle Paul wrote to Timothy saying:

*'Hold fast the **pattern** of sound words which you have heard from me, in faith and love which are in Christ Jesus.'*

(2 Timothy 1:12,13)

By building his life according to God's principles, the righteous man in Psalm 112 established the course for his 'descendants to be mighty on the earth.' This speaks of a people who are strong, influential and making a difference in the world.

Have you ever stopped to consider the pattern your life is setting for the generations following you? The Bible says:

'A good man leaves an inheritance for his children's children.'

(Proverbs 13:22)

A great legacy to leave your children or grandchildren goes way beyond a house or a lump sum of money. A great legacy is the successful example of your life, which enables them to build on the foundation you have laid. As I wrote in my book *You Can Change The Future*, our capacity to live powerful and effective lives can transcend our own and impact future generations.

'I have been young, and now am old; yet I have not seen the righteous forsaken, nor his descendants begging bread. He is ever merciful, and lends; and his descendants are blessed.' (Psalm 37: 25,26)

The promise of God for a righteous life is that the blessing on your life will be passed on to your descendants.

> 'THE GENERATION OF THE UPRIGHT WILL BE BLESSED.'
>
> [PSALM 112:2]

GENERATIONS

God always works through generations. From generation to generation, blessing and curses are being passed on. Look back at your own family tree, and you may discover what blessings (or problems and negative characteristics, for that matter) you have inherited.

The good news is that no matter what your background or heritage, not only can you change the course of your life, but you can set a new course for the generations ahead. The moment you give your life to Jesus Christ is the moment a new spiritual heritage begins. The Bible says:

'Train up a child in the way he should go, and when he is old he will not depart from it.' (Proverbs 22:6)

A child will grow up in the way they were trained or raised. This works both positively and negatively. You can see the fruit of Biblical principles when they become the foundation of a young person's life. They have purpose, confidence, great attitudes, and are becoming successful. On the other hand, you can see the deterioration of generations when Christ and His principles are rejected or compromised.

The choices you make today have the power to change the future. The righteous man in Psalm 112 imparted something powerful to his children – the wisdom and principles of God that enabled them to live blessed lives.

When you live according to God's principles, you are passing on God's blessing to future generations.

> 'WEALTH AND RICHES WILL BE IN HIS HOUSE.'
>
> [PSALM 112:3]

PROSPERITY

Another promise of God is that wealth and riches will be in your house. I know there are those who would be more comfortable if the verse said wealth and riches will be in his *heart* rather than in his *house*. They are the ones who wrestle with the fact that prosperity is the promise of God for their lives.

It is amazing that so many Christians feel guilty about wealth. Sadly, this kind of poverty-thinking has been a curse to the Church because it presumes that wealth and greed are the same thing, and this limits resourcefulness. 'Prosperity' is a word frequently found in the Bible; so are the words 'blessing', 'wealth', 'riches' and 'abundance.' I cannot find any scripture that states it is God's will for us to be poor and destitute. For instance, the Word of God says:

> *'Let the Lord be magnified, who has **pleasure in the prosperity** of His servant.'* (Psalm 35: 27)

Think about that – God rejoices when we prosper. The impact of our prosperity is enlarged and finds its purpose when we get the revelation that His blessing in our lives has others as its focus.

Our Heavenly Father, like any loving parent, does not mind if His children prosper. But bear in mind that wealth and riches are just one aspect of prosperity – it goes further than material goods. John wrote:

> *'Beloved, I pray that you may prosper in **all things** and be in health, just as your soul prospers.'* (3 John 1:2)

Money cannot buy family, great relationships, a good reputation or your physical well-being. Don't under-estimate or exclude these blessings from your definition of prosperity. A truly prosperous person desires the fullness of God in every area of their life.

> 'AND HIS RIGHTEOUSNESS ENDURES FOREVER.'
>
> [PSALM 112:3]

RIGHTEOUSNESS

Never lose sight of the fact that God desires to bless you. It is interesting to note how often 'righteousness' and the principles of blessing are mentioned together in the Bible.

I don't believe money is a problem with God because it is a tremendous resource for good – but the Bible consistently confronts a person's **attitude** towards money. It says that *'the love of money* is the root of all kinds of evil' (1 Timothy 6:10). The purposes of your heart will distinguish whether your money has the potential for righteousness or unrighteousness. The Word of God says:

> *'For no sooner has the sun risen with a burning heat than it withers the grass; its flower falls, and its beautiful appearance perishes. So the rich man also will fade away in his **pursuits**.'*
>
> (James 1:11)

The problem isn't in the rich man's wealth, but in what his heart is pursuing. If your pursuits are focusing only on your needs and your desires, then it is temporal and will fade away. But Jesus instructed us quite clearly what we should pursue:

> *'But **seek first the Kingdom of God and His righteousness**, and all these things shall be added to you.'* (Matthew 6:33)

The key here is what you put FIRST and what your priorities in life are. When you put God's Kingdom first in your life and pursue His righteousness, His promise is that 'these things' – your material needs such as food or clothing – will be met. Making His Kingdom your priority means you sow into something that has eternal value and will not fade away. As the Bible declares, '... and his righteousness endures forever.'

> 'UNTO THE UPRIGHT THERE ARISES LIGHT IN THE DARKNESS.'
>
> [PSALM 112:4]

HELP IN TROUBLE

We will all face challenges in our lives – be it financial pressures, work and health issues, or relationship challenges. One of the great blessings in life is that no matter what we are going through, we are never alone. The Bible says:

*'God is our refuge and strength, a very **present help** in trouble.'*

(Psalm 46:1)

King David, the writer of 'The Lord is my shepherd,' knew the 'present help' of God. In Psalm 23, he wrote, 'Though I walk through the valley of the shadow of death, I shall fear no evil for You are with me.' He also wrote, 'My heart also instructs me in the night seasons' (Psalm 16:7).

There are many things that thrive in the darkness of night, such as confusion, anxiety and fear. Many have lost their way in dark times, but the promise to the righteous man in Psalm 112 is that in the midst of darkness, there arises a light. Throughout the Bible, the analogy of light is always representative of God. Jesus is called the Light of the world, and light always dispels the darkness.

Our challenge is to stand strong and remain consistent when we face the 'dark times.' If, as David said, it is our heart that instructs us in these times, then we need to set our heart on the promises of God. If all your heart knows is panic, then that is the instruction it will give you, and you will feel helpless and powerless in a time of trouble.

In the midst of a crisis, remain faithful and diligent. Stand firmly on the Word of God, ask Him to guide you, and you will eventually see the darkness disperse. Remember, God is 'a very present help in trouble.'

> 'HE IS GRACIOUS, AND FULL OF COMPASSION, AND RIGHTEOUS.'
>
> [PSALM 112:4]

GRACE AND COMPASSION

The righteous man in Psalm 112 is described as someone who is gracious and full of compassion. These two powerful qualities are also attributes of Jesus Christ.

You may have heard the words of the well-known song *Amazing Grace* and wondered what was so amazing about grace? God's grace is His favour; it is unmerited and bountiful in supply. It is a free gift. Some people can't accept that grace is enough – they want to do something more to earn it themselves.

*'Where sin abounds, **grace** abounds much more.'* (Romans 5:29)

You may have made some great mistakes in your life, but these do not have to dominate your future if you understand that God's grace prevails even more. There is nothing more you need to do, other than make the decision to turn your life around and accept His unmerited favour and undeserved blessing. When you have an understanding of God's grace, you can accept His blessing in your life.

Compassion is another powerful characteristic. Every time Jesus was moved with compassion, something powerful happened.

*'And when Jesus went out He saw a great multitude; and He was **moved with compassion** for them.'* (Matthew 14:14)

When facing a tough situation, human nature is easily drawn to sympathy, but the reality is that sympathy is not always what is needed. Sympathy identifies with the problem or hurt, and may make you feel better for a time, but it is not focussed on helping you move forward.

People tend to surround themselves with those who 'understand them' or 'accept them just the way they are,' rather than positioning themselves in a challenging environment that will direct them towards answers. Sympathy doesn't have any answers, but compassion is a powerful force that activates God's answers for your life.

> 'A GOOD MAN DEALS GRACIOUSLY AND LENDS.'
>
> [PSALM 112:5]

DEALING GRACIOUSLY

God's promise is that we should be the lender and not the borrower (see Deuteronomy 28:12). If you are always in need, you are poorly positioned to help others. It is far better to be well positioned to lend or give to others, than to constantly be on the receiving end. The Bible describes it in this way:

> *'The rich rules over the poor, and the borrower is servant to the lender.'* (Proverbs 22:7)

Commit yourself to a journey in which you progress from being the borrower or the receiver, to being the lender or supplier. Ownership puts you in a position to bless other people's lives – it gives you this opportunity because you cannot give what you do not own. It isn't about you controlling others but protecting **you** from being the subject of manipulation or control. If you are always taking or borrowing, it imprisons or binds you, but when you are in the position to give, it releases you.

While the world is often on the take with ruthless wheelings and dealings, a Godly person should act fairly and be gracious in their dealings. This includes the way they do business, and the way they deal with people and relationships. It also affects the way they respond to hurt and offences.

If you want to know how to deal graciously, just think about how God deals with those who choose to follow Him – with an immeasurable supply of grace. When it comes to relationships or business, make a commitment to be open and honest. God is unlikely to bless shady dealings or dishonesty. Have integrity when it comes to finances, and treat others with grace and generosity. Working within the right principles and parameters will not only bless you, but those you deal with will experience the blessing too.

> 'HE WILL GUIDE
> HIS AFFAIRS
> WITH
> DISCRETION.'
>
> [PSALM 112:5]

GUIDED BY DISCRETION

The Word says that the Psalm 112 man guides his affairs with discretion. To be guided means to be directed, led or steered towards a specific course. Some people aren't guided by anything – they are tossed around by circumstances, but Jesus said:

*'When He, the Spirit of Truth, has come, He will **guide** you into all truth.'* (John 16:13)

You will always have many options available to you in life, but God's way will always steer you in the direction of His purposes.

Why should you be guided by discretion? The Word of God says:

'Discretion will preserve you; understanding will keep you.'

(Proverbs 2:11)

Discretion will keep you on course. Conducting your affairs with discretion will protect you from the consequences of hasty or bad decisions. It includes dealing graciously, having integrity and using Godly wisdom.

To have discretion also means to be blessed with good taste and good sense. There are some who have great taste but no sense, and others who have good sense but no taste. For example, if you were to buy a beautiful luxury car which you couldn't afford – you have great taste but no sense. (Some choose a car which shows good sense but no taste!) A young man's choice of a beautiful bride may show impeccable taste, but if he ignores or mistreats her, he lacks good sense. He'll never have the marriage he dreams about.

I believe you can have both by guiding your affairs according to the Word of God and listening to your conscience. Approach your life wisely, with good judgement, and live a life of blessing.

> 'SURELY HE WILL NEVER BE SHAKEN.'
>
> [PSALM 112:6]

UNSHAKEABLE

One of the certainties in the life of the Psalm 112 man is that he will 'never be shaken.' It doesn't say that he won't experience times of 'shaking' but the promise of God is that he won't be shaken loose. Why? Because he is firmly fixed in position, or as these verses say, his heart is steadfast and established.

How easily can you be shaken? The truth is you will never know until you feel the shaking. In December 1989, a destructive earthquake hit the New South Wales city of Newcastle. I had stayed there on occasion in a particular modern hotel, but after the earthquake, that building ceased to exist. On the outside, it appeared to be the building least likely to fall in an earthquake, but it was completely ruined.

Why is it that some people are destroyed by shaky times and others emerge strong and victorious? It all depends on where their heart is **set** and established. The psalmist wrote:

*'I have **set** the Lord always before me, because He is at my right hand I shall not be moved.'* (Psalm 16:8)

In the same way a plane flies according to a **set** computerised flight plan, your life operates according to the way your heart is **set**. When you are feeling disappointment or your faith is being tested, what is inside your heart will come out. If your heart is not **set** or established on the right foundation, your life will veer off course.

What you really believe will come out in the midst of adversity. Jesus said that from the abundance of the heart the mouth speaks. It is easy to sing praises to God and speak positively when everything is going well, but what comes out when you are facing a crisis? When your heart is established and set according to God's Word, you may feel tremors along the way, but you won't be shaken loose or go off course.

> 'THE RIGHTEOUS WILL BE IN EVERLASTING REMEMBRANCE.'
>
> [PSALM 112:6]

LASTING LEGACY

Have you ever wondered what kind of name you will leave behind when you have departed from this earth? A good name, a bad name, or no name?

Leaving behind a good name for your children is a great inheritance, instead of the liability of a bad name with a bad reputation. Your name is something your descendants should be proud to bear and wear like a badge of honour. The Word says:

> 'The **memory** of the righteous is blessed but the name of the wicked will rot.' (Proverbs 10:7)

Earlier, we looked at the power of impacting the future generations, but in serving the future, we cannot neglect to serve the present.

A blessed life is one that understands that when God saves you, He has others in mind. I believe every Christian needs to know that they are not only *saved*, but are also *called* to live a life of purpose.

'*[God] who has **saved** us and **called** us with a holy calling*'

(2 Timothy 1:9)

One of the greatest things we can contribute to in our lives is in building what Jesus said He would build – His Church. He said the gates of hell will not prevail against His Church, so our commitment to the establishment and prosperity of His Church brings our life into line with His will.

One of the greatest decisions you can make is to choose to live a life that is dedicated to accomplishing and building something that will stand as a testimony or legacy for the generations ahead.

> 'HE WILL NOT BE AFRAID OF EVIL TIDINGS.'
>
> [PSALM 112:7]

NO WORRIES

I once taught a series of messages entitled 'What a worry worry is.' It is amazing how much time people spend worrying – about their work, relationships, money or health.

Do you know that the very sound of a telephone ringing can strike fear into the heart of a person who is fearful of bad news, and cause their heart to sink? Inevitably, that anxiety will begin to rule their life and affect them physically, emotionally and spiritually. The truth is that worry will always hold you back and limit your potential. It never achieves anything positive, because it always focuses on the problem instead of the answers. This is what the Bible says:

'Anxiety in the heart causes depression, but a good word makes it glad.' (Proverbs 12:25)

In the face of life's challenges, surround yourself with positive, faith-filled words that challenge the problem and focus on answers. Your environment is critical at such times. Carefully choose your friends, your counsel, and your place of worship. Avoid those whose belief system is devoid of answers for life's everyday problems. Never accept the mindset that persecution and suffering are the will of God; they are the weapons of the devil who is hell-bent on distracting you from God's amazing plan for your life.

While he would prefer you to become consumed with negativity, it is the will of God for you to fill your life with a good report. Anxiety, worry and fear will rob you of faith and hope, and ultimately prevent you from moving forward with God. The words 'Do not fear' are a frequent instruction in scripture, and it says *'be anxious for nothing'* (Philippians 4:6). If you are living according to God's principles of peace and prosperity, you need never be afraid of bad news. Even when a bad report comes, it will not rule your life.

> 'HIS HEART IS STEADFAST, TRUSTING IN THE LORD.'
>
> [PSALM 112:7]

STEADFASTNESS AND TRUST

One of the advantages of having a vibrant faith is steadfastness. To be steadfast involves a refusal to be swayed or moved from your course. It is sheer determination, and the ability to stand firm against all odds. You don't have to live on an emotional roller coaster if your life is founded on a genuine faith in God.

The first pastor of the Corinthian Church was the Apostle Paul who challenged the early Christians to be steadfast:

*'Be **steadfast**, immovable, always abounding in the work of the Lord, knowing that your labour is not in vain.'* (1 Corinthians 15:58)

The 1st Century Christians stood firm in the midst of persecution, and as a result, they experienced tremendous increase and progress.

Psalm 112 links steadfastness to trusting God. The righteous man in Psalm 112 has great wealth and riches, but his heart isn't trusting in them – his trust is in the Lord. Faith and trust such as this will produce steadfastness and stability in your life.

To put your trust in someone or something means you will have a firm belief in their reliability, and a confident expectation that they will not let you down. Such dependability is the outcome of a vibrant relationship with the Almighty God. He is called El Shaddai, which means 'more than enough' – ever dependable, always steadfast. He is the foundation of a steadfast spirit that will cause you to be forward-focused and immovably persistent. This is what the Bible says:

*'**Trust** in the Lord with all your heart, and lean not on your own understanding. In all your ways acknowledge Him and He shall direct your paths.'* (Proverbs 3:5,6)

When you trust God with your whole life, you need never be anxious or afraid. He will never let you down.

'HIS HEART IS ESTABLISHED.'

[PSALM 112:8]

CONVICTIONS

You may wonder why there are those whose lives follow a pattern of crisis and inconsistency, while others live according to a pattern of blessing and good fortune. It's simple – those with *strong convictions* build strength into their life, but those who have weak convictions, weaken their lives. It all depends where one's heart is set.

The truth is, if you stand for nothing, you will fall for anything! You cannot be neutral – you have to make a stand. The Apostle Paul knew what he stood for, and nothing could sway him from his convictions. From his prison cell, he wrote of what he knew and believed, of his persuasion and commitment to Jesus Christ.

*'Nevertheless I am not ashamed, for **I know** whom **I have believed** and **am persuaded** that He is able to keep what I **have committed** to Him until that Day.'* (2 Timothy 1:12)

There are many who don't know what their convictions are – they are unsure about what they believe. Instead of being influential or persuasive, they are easily influenced by whatever comes their way.

Your persuasion or convictions determine your course in life. The result is that you will either be someone who lives with *conviction*, or someone who lives by *consequence*.

*'There is a way that **seems** right to a man, but its end is the way of death.'* (Proverbs 16:25)

A lack of conviction will not kill you physically, but it may lead to the death of your dreams, your marriage or your well-being. Living by consequence means putting your trust in what *seems* right, but living with conviction is living according to what *is* right – living God's way!

You need to know what your convictions are because they are the beliefs and principles that will establish a pattern for your life.

'HE WILL NOT BE AFRAID, UNTIL HE SEES HIS DESIRE UPON HIS ENEMIES.'

[PSALM 112:8]

SUCCESS

A blessed life is one that will know success, not failure. Success, like prosperity, is a Bible word. In Joshua 1:8, the promise of God is that living by the principles of the Bible will 'make your way prosperous and give you good success.' As discussed earlier, to achieve that success means meditating on the Word of God and living according to His principles.

Some people think it is a formula – that God will wave a magic wand and they will begin to prosper. However, you cannot approach the blessing of God with some sort of 'penny-in-the-slot' mentality, thinking, 'If I do this, God has to do that.'

Some people become discouraged when they don't see breakthrough immediately, but the faithfulness of God isn't proven in a week or a month. You need to have a life-long approach to His principles.

You may look at some well-known, successful people and want what they have. But instead of only looking at their position now, you need to consider what it took to get them there. Many people want the blessing and promise, but they don't want to work for it or wait for it. The Word of God says:

'Imitate those who through faith and patience inherit the promises.'

(Hebrews 6:12)

People with great potential have sabotaged their opportunity because they lacked the patience to endure in the tough times. You will need staying power if you want to live a blessed life. If you don't experience success straight away, don't give up. Keep on doing the will of God with a spirit of patience and endurance. He has given you all you need to fulfill His plan and purpose for your life, and if you constantly put God first, you can trust Him to fulfill His promise to bless you.

> 'HE HAS DISPERSED ABROAD.'
>
> [PSALM 112:9]

VISION

One of the things I love about this righteous man in Psalm 112 is that he clearly lives a life that goes well beyond himself. When it says, 'he has dispersed abroad,' it speaks of one whose life has a far-reaching and wide-ranging impact on others.

There are those who never seem to move forward in life because their vision is small. Instead of continuing to grow and expand their life, they prefer to be a big fish in a small pond. In doing so, they limit their own potential. The Bible says:

'Where there is no vision, the people perish.' (Proverbs 29:18)

Having a dream or specific goal will add direction and purpose to your life. There are so many people who are frustrated because they aren't going anywhere or achieving anything. Their time, their energy and their finance is wasted because their life lacks purpose.

In my book *For This Cause*, I wrote about the words of Jesus – He knew that He was born for the Cause of God's Kingdom, and understood that His connection to the world revolved around that Cause. You and I are also born for the Cause, which involves living a life with influence that goes well beyond yourself.

It is easy to get caught up in the stress and pressure of your job, working to pay the bills and to put food on your table. But with a big-hearted spirit, you begin to think about dispersing abroad in terms of what you can do for others, and putting food on many other tables. It is impossible to have a vision that is bigger than God's plans for your life. His plans are HUGE. As God begins to bless your life, keep expanding and looking beyond yourself to build His Kingdom. The world is your oyster!

> 'HE HAS
> GIVEN TO
> THE POOR.'
>
> [PSALM 112:9]

GENEROSITY

God's nature is to give, and everything He does comes from a generous spirit. In the same way, we should desire to be truly generous and allow our lives to be a flow of blessing to others. Generosity isn't about how much you have, nor is it proven in a single act – the true spirit of generosity is a lifestyle.

• A way of seeing

*'He who has a **generous eye** will be blessed for he gives of his bread to the poor.'* (Proverbs 22:9)

A generous eye will see beyond itself and quickly spot opportunities to bless others. Instead of being someone who sits back and makes harsh judgements about others, a generous spirit will be open to believe the best.

• A way of thinking

*'But a generous man **devises generous things**.'* (Isaiah 32:8)

When generosity is a way of thinking, one will always be devising plans to bless others. God saw the need of the world and He devised a generous strategy. It is called the Gospel, which means 'good news.'

• A way of living

'And by generosity he shall stand.' (Isaiah 32:8)

When generosity is a way of living, it becomes our stance. It is not a labour, a single action or a grudging obligation – it is a way of life. The promise of God is that one who has a 'generous eye' is someone who will be blessed themselves.

God's Kingdom refers to everything within His realm, both in Heaven and on earth. To have a Kingdom spirit means you have a vision that is bigger than you – you will always be devising generous strategies or plans to bless others. Generosity will be a way of seeing, a way of thinking, and a way of living.

> 'HIS RIGHTEOUSNESS ENDURES FOREVER.'
>
> [PSALM 112:9]

ENDURANCE

The promises of God are readily available to you, but you will need a commitment to endurance, persistence and patience to see them established. The Bible tells us:

*'You have need of **endurance** so that after you have done the will of God you may receive the promise.'* (Hebrews 10:36)

Endurance is about the refusal to surrender, and the determination to keep on going until you receive the promise. Once you decide you want to live a life built on the principles of God, you may face opposition and persecution, as well as the temptation to quit. James wrote:

*'Blessed is the man who **endures** temptation; for when he has been approved, he will receive the crown of life.'* (James 1:12)

The Bible is full of encouragement to stand strong in the face of adversity. James continued in his letter, pointing out that *'when'* we are tempted (not *if)*, it does not come from God. He went on to describe how temptation starts when people are enticed by their own desires, or quite literally, deceitful representations, which paint an unrealistic picture that does not exist. My wife Bobbie and I once visited Florence in Italy, and when we checked into our hotel, the room looked nothing like the one in the brochure. When querying this, the hotel front desk told us, 'That's just a picture' – the room did not exist!

In the face of discouragement, be wary of illusions that form in your mind which make quitting or compromising look attractive. Such a picture does not tell the whole story and is part of Satan's strategy to rob you of God's blessing. A spirit of endurance is about commitment to the long haul – and you will need it when it comes to your marriage, your finances and even your spiritual walk with God. When the going gets tough, don't look for short-cuts or the easy way out.

> 'HIS HORN
> WILL BE
> EXALTED WITH
> HONOUR.'
>
> [PSALM 112:9]

RESPECT

Psalm 112 describes how the righteous man's 'horn will be exalted with honour.' In Bible terms, his 'horn' refers to his strength and influence, and to be 'honoured' is all about others recognising his value. It literally means that his influence is elevated through credibility and respect, causing him to rise to high power and a place of honour.

It is clear that respect is part of God's blessing, and is a tremendous advantage in living a life of influence. The Word says that Godly wisdom will lead to ...

'... favour and high esteem in the sight of God and man.' (Proverbs 3:4)

Think about what it means to have favour and to be held in high esteem by both God and others. Such a person would be one who had good character and great influence.

So why would respect be a blessing in your life? You can be successful in what you do, but without respect, you can never reach any significant level of influence. Here are five things respect will add to your life:

- Your words will have authority.
- Prosperity will follow you.
- Promotion will be a way of life.
- Respect will protect you from rumours and attack.
- People will rally to your cause.

Respect is not a luxury that can be bought. It is not something you can demand, but rather something you earn over time. The truth is that if you want to gain respect, you need to give respect. No matter what God has called you to do, giving honour and gaining respect will help you achieve it.

'THE WICKED WILL SEE IT AND BE GRIEVED.'

[PSALM 112:10]

PROTECTION

Respect will protect you against unexpected attacks from your adversaries. For centuries, one of Satan's strategies has been to destroy the credibility of Christians and undermine the reputation of the Church.

Losing your credibility can render you ineffective because you can also lose the authority, prosperity and position of influence you may have gained. Having integrity, righteousness and respect are a great protection against the weapons of your enemy, the devil. The promise in the Word of God is:

> *'No weapon formed against you shall prosper, and every tongue which rises against you in judgement you shall condemn. This is the heritage of the servants of the Lord.'* (Isaiah 54:17)

Weapons may be formed against you, but they certainly won't be successful, unless *you* make yourself an easy target. The Bible clearly instructs us:

> *'Nor give place to the devil.'* (Ephesians 4:27)

Giving him no opportunity, no advantage and no permission to move in your life is how you thwart his attempts to rob you of the blessing of God.

To be a skillful tennis player, you have to cut off the angles, making it difficult for your opponent to get a shot past you. This is how you can thwart the strategies of the devil – cut off the angles and don't be ignorant of his devices. Satan will never play fair. If there are issues in your life that give him room to move, deal with them. If you don't, you are giving him opportunity to use them against you. You can close the door on him and bullet-proof your marriage, your emotions, your health and your finances by living according to God's principles.

> 'HE WILL GNASH HIS TEETH AND MELT AWAY.'
>
> [PSALM 112:10]

PERSECUTION

I mentioned earlier how the Amplified Bible describes 'blessed' as 'happy, fortunate and *to be envied.*' The reality is that when God begins to bless your life, not everyone will be happy about it.

The blessing of God is enviable and can cause some to 'gnash their teeth.' Along with the blessing of prosperity and success, you can expect to face opposition. When you put God first, this is what Jesus said you can expect:

> *'Assuredly, I say to you, there is no one who has left house or brothers or sisters or father or mother or wife or children or lands, for My sake and the Gospel's, who shall not receive a hundredfold now in this time – houses and brothers and sisters and mothers and children and lands, **with persecutions** – and in the age to come, eternal life.'* (Mark 10: 29,30)

When we make a stand for God, we should never be surprised if we attract opposition or persecution. The devil is always seeking to steal, kill and destroy, but persecution will also come from a minority who feel threatened by God's blessing. For instance, Jesus faced persecution from kings who thought their kingdom was under threat, from crowds who realised their mediocrity was threatened, and religious leaders who sensed their legalistic beliefs were under threat. A blessed life will attract attention from those who will attempt to pull you down to size – their size!

When your life is impacted by God, you clearly have what others want. In the midst of persecution, refuse to draw back or allow others to rule your spirit. 'Having done all, stand' and keep your course.

> 'THE DESIRE OF THE WICKED SHALL PERISH.'
>
> [PSALM 112:10]

VICTORY

The final sentence that describes the life of the righteous man in Psalm 112 states that 'the desire of the wicked shall perish' or come to nothing. In other words, the desire (or plans and purposes) of God will stand. What a triumphant conclusion to a blessed life. The promise in God's Word is:

> *'He who has begun a good work in you will complete it unto the day of Jesus Christ.'* (Philippians 1:6)

God is committed to seeing you succeed and He desires to complete what He has started in your life. Your faith will be tested and there will be times when you will face the temptation to abandon the principles of God, but the key is to take on the spirit of an overcomer. This is how an overcomer will approach life:

> *'And let us not grow weary while doing good for in due season we shall reap if we do not lose heart.'* (Galatians 6:9)

This verse reveals five characteristics of an overcomer:

- **They refuse to grow weary**. At times they may be physically tired yet they are still energised by vision, focus and opportunity in life.

- **They continue to do good**. Whether or not they have a good start, an overcomer will be determined to finish well.

- **They recognise their season is due** (perhaps even overdue).

- **They are committed to reaping**, according to the good seed they have sown. Sow good seed and you can expect to reap accordingly.

- **An overcomer is determined not to lose heart**.

The adversary's plan is to hold you back from the blessing of God, and prevent you from reaching your goal and living a quality life. But John encourages us that *'He who is in you is greater than he who is in the world'* (1 John 4:4).

Praise the Lord! Blessed is the man who fears the Lord, who delights greatly in His commandments. ² His descendants will be mighty on earth; The generation of the upright will be blessed. ³ Wealth and riches will be in his house, and his righteousness endures forever. ⁴ Unto the upright there arises light in the darkness; He is gracious, and full of compassion, and righteous. ⁵ A good man deals graciously and lends; He will guide his affairs with discretion. ⁶ Surely he will never be shaken; The righteous will be in everlasting remembrance. ⁷ He will not be afraid of evil tidings; His heart is steadfast, trusting in the Lord. ⁸ His heart is established; He will not be afraid, until he sees his desire upon his enemies. ⁹ He has dispersed abroad, He has given to the poor; His righteousness endures forever; His horn will be exalted with honour. ¹⁰ The wicked will see it and be grieved; He will gnash his teeth and melt away; The desire of the wicked will perish. Praise the Lord! Blessed is the man who fears the Lord, who delights greatly in His commandments. ² His descendants will be mighty on earth; The generation of the upright will be blessed. ³ Wealth and riches will be in his house, and his righteousness endures forever. ⁴ Unto the upright there arises light in the darkness; He is gracious, and full of compassion, and righteous. ⁵ A good man deals graciously and lends; He will guide his affairs with discretion. ⁶ Surely he will never be shaken; The righteous will be in everlasting remembrance. ⁷ He will not be afraid of evil tidings; His heart is steadfast, trusting in the Lord. ⁸ His heart is established; He will not be afraid, until he sees his desire upon his enemies. ⁹ He has dispersed abroad, He has given to the poor; His righteousness endures forever; His horn will be exalted with honour. ¹⁰ The wicked will see it and be grieved; He will gnash his teeth and melt away; The desire of the wicked will perish. Praise the Lord! Blessed is the man who fears the Lord, who delights greatly in His commandments. ² His descendants will be mighty on earth; The generation of the upright will be blessed. ³ Wealth and riches will be in his house, and his righteousness endures forever. ⁴ Unto the upright there arises light in the darkness; He is gracious, and full of compassion, and righteous. ⁵ A good man deals graciously and lends; He will guide his affairs with discretion. ⁶ Surely he will never be shaken; The righteous will be in everlasting remembrance. ⁷ He will not be afraid of evil tidings; His heart is steadfast, trusting in the Lord. ⁸ His heart is established; He will not be afraid, until he sees his desire upon his enemies. ⁹ He has dispersed abroad, He has given to the poor; His righteousness endures forever; His horn will be exalted with honour. ¹⁰ The wicked will see it and be grieved; He will gnash his teeth and melt away; The desire of the wicked will perish. Praise the Lord! Blessed is the man who fears the Lord, who delights greatly in His commandments. ² His descendants will be mighty on earth; The generation of the upright will be blessed. ³ Wealth and riches will be in his house, and his righteousness endures forever. ⁴ Unto the upright there arises light in the darkness; He is gracious, and full of compassion, and righteous. ⁵ A good man deals graciously and lends; He will guide his affairs with discretion. ⁶ S

EPILOGUE

I'm sure you will agree with me that the lifestyle of the righteous man in Psalm 112 is one we should all aspire to. The principles and commandments of God are evident right across the spectrum of his life. He has it all.

He puts God first in his life, he lives according to the Bible and as a result he is successful and prosperous. He also has a far-sighted sense of purpose that extends well beyond himself. He gives generously to others; his family is blessed; he is making his mark and he is highly respected. Like anyone else, he faces his share of tests, trials, challenges and temptations, but he comes through victorious.

But there is more ... not only is his life blessed, but his character is outstanding. He loves God, he is righteous, generous, just, gracious, compassionate, wise and full of integrity. He is someone we would all be drawn to and aspire to be like. Yet there is one final truth about this man.

When you turn over the page, you will read the psalm that precedes Psalm 112. Psalm 111 is a wonderful description of the awesome nature and character of God, but the amazing thing is that the psalmist has used exactly the same phrases to describe the character of the righteous man in Psalm 112. Not only does the righteous man experience blessing in every area of his life but his character is likened to God's – 'gracious', 'full of compassion' with a 'righteousness that endures forever.'

This righteous, blessed man may not be named, but I think there is a good reason for that. We all have the opportunity to be that person, and as we begin to live according to the principles of the Bible, we can put our own name to those ten verses.

May you live a blessed life.

PSALM 111

Praise the Lord! I will praise the Lord with my whole heart, in the assembly of the upright and in the congregation.

2 The works of the Lord are great, studied by all who have pleasure in them.

3 His work is honorable and glorious, and His righteousness endures forever.

4 He has made His wonderful works to be remembered; the Lord is gracious and full of compassion.

5 He has given food to those who fear Him; He will ever be mindful of His covenant.

6 He has declared to His people the power of His works, in giving them the heritage of the nations.

7 The works of His hands are verity and justice; all His precepts are sure.

8 They stand fast forever and ever, and are done in truth and uprightness.

9 He has sent redemption to His people; He has commanded His covenant forever: holy and awesome is His name.

10 The fear of the Lord is the beginning of wisdom; a good understanding have all those who do His commandments. His praise endures forever.

BOOKS BY BRIAN HOUSTON

GET A LIFE
PRINCIPLES FOR SUCCESS AND ENJOYMENT
IN EVERY AREA OF LIFE

YOU NEED MORE MONEY
DISCOVERING GOD'S AMAZING FINANCIAL PLAN
FOR YOUR LIFE

YOU CAN CHANGE THE FUTURE
LIVING BEYOND TODAY AND IMPACTING
THE GENERATIONS AHEAD

FOR THIS CAUSE
FINDING THE MEANING OF LIFE, AND
LIVING A LIFE OF MEANING

BOOKS BY BOBBIE HOUSTON

I'LL HAVE WHAT SHE'S HAVING
THE ULTIMATE COMPLIMENT TO ANY WOMAN DARING TO
LOOK LIFE IN THE FACE

HEAVEN IS IN THIS HOUSE